KEYS TO HAVE FINANCIAL BREAKTHROUGH: Amazing ways on How to stay financially strong.

Melvin F. Babcock

Table of contents

Chapter 1

How to find the best paying job

Job hunting has devolved into a dog-eat-dog game! The desire for high-paying occupations that can put food on the table and allow for purchasing certain "luxuries" is ubiquitous. When seeking a good job, relevant skills are more vital than credentials.

There is nothing wrong with wishing for a well-paying job. Employees will always believe that fairly compensated is critical to their overall job satisfaction. Unfortunately, the minimum wage is inadequate. Individuals earning the minimum wage must reduce spending and make do with their modest salaries.
Some form of insecurity constantly plagues people who live from hand to mouth. The

future appears dismal since most people need to learn how to live after they retire. As a result, it is easy to understand why people virtually always desire better salaries.

How can you get some of the Highest Paying Jobs to help you secure your future? There is, however, a method to locating and recruiting High Paying Jobs. As you read on, I'll reveal the secret.

Do you have hard and soft skills and are looking for a high-paying job? Make a solid CV to land a high-paying job.

Those who live on a little income are more vulnerable to insecurity. Most individuals will have to learn to survive once they retire, so the future is bleak. As a result, it's easy to see why people continually demand higher pay. There is a way to attract and obtain high-paying jobs. How can you get some of the highest-paying jobs that will help you secure your financial future? I'll reveal the secret as you read on.

Do you have hard and soft skills and are looking for a high-paying job?

Are you ready to discover more about where to hunt for the highest-paying jobs anywhere in the world? Do it right now! In the next five minutes, we'll discuss what separates people who earn significantly more than the minimum wage from those who don't.

How to Get the Highest-Paying Jobs in Seven Simple Steps

Improve Your Expert Status

People are willing to pay a high price to hire professionals to execute jobs. This is especially true when people understand they cannot do what they can. Consider a surgeon who is paid to do life-saving surgery or a lawyer who is born to get someone released.

However, if you establish yourself as an expert in a particular field, people will gladly give you the amount you demand.

You can take a variety of approaches. To make oneself more appealing to higher pay, you should focus on creating and presenting yourself as an authority figure. Because they know this, the government and other labor employers will agree to pay you a fair wage.

Look for speaking opportunities at various conventions.
Regularly write on social media and provide consulting services (part-time).
When applied collectively, these activities can help you land the highest-paying job.

You Care About the Environment
Your geographic location is critical for landing a well-paying job. There is a catch, even though high living standards can be found in highly developed places. If you prefer to live in a rural area with little to do, you may have to accept a ridiculous wage. However, staying in the country's most developed locations increases your chances of getting better-paying work...

Your immediate surroundings extend beyond where you dwell. Your social circle and local network are also taken into account. If you have the right network, it will be easier for you to stay up to current on valuable information about employment opportunities.

They can get you a job in a wealthy field or, at the absolute least, inspire you to greatness. Your chances of becoming a local champion grow if you are among other customers.

Create a Powerful Network
You must build a strong network and maintain favorable relationships with the people in it. This method is still quite effective even if you remain in a confining environment. Like literature, the internet serves as a window to the globe, eliminating borders and bringing people together. LinkedIn is a professional networking

website that allows you to connect with achievers from all walks of life.

You must be intelligent and cautious when positioning yourself for opportunities. You must also be prepared to seize opportunities as they arise. Never underestimate the power of a few words here and there. Make good use of your social media platforms! Connect with people in that field if you want to work there, but make sure you do so.

Carry out research

As a form of study, your presence here for a well-paying career is strongly suggested. To attain your objectives, you must research and ask critical questions. Search the internet, speak with friends, read books, and learn about lucrative opportunities outside your sector.

By completing research, you can uncover online forums where members can access insider news, updates, and job openings.

Take advantage of every opportunity you come across! You may join a Telegram group that regularly updates information about job openings in a given industry. Finding a job on such networks that pays a respectable hourly or monthly rate is simple. You are less likely to be scammed in a well-organized, strictly controlled community.

Prudent Risk-Taking

If you want to boost your pay significantly, you'll need to take intelligent risks. It would help to move outside of your comfort zone to take calculated risks. If you see a position that interests you, apply straight away. You must overcome entry barriers and use them even if you do not appear qualified for enticing job offers. Apply for the highest-paying employment, even if it seems unattainable.

Everyone wants a problem solver for their team. Turn become one! You'll get further if you can offer your potential employer examples of issues you've solved. Consider your distinctive contributions as well as how you portray and promote yourself.

Improve your CV to stand out!
Your resume must be updated and polished to perfection. You can get aid from CV specialists because they are aware of the necessary changes to make. Of course, your resume must be available during your job search.

To be recognized, you must, like earlier parts, endeavor to stand out. Aiming for maximum visibility, you may ensure that as many hiring managers as possible notice your qualifications. This boosts your chances of landing your dream job.

You can send your CV to some of the largest and most prominent hiring agencies in the United States, and they will connect you with businesses and opportunities that interest you. Several well-known corporations frequently interact with recruiters to gain access to qualified candidates for critical posts. As a result, you will receive job alerts when these positions become available.

Rest assured.
You must be self-assured and have a positive attitude in life. If you lack confidence, you risk missing out on many excellent opportunities. Indeed, you have to believe it before you see it.

Finally, you must always provide value to both yourself and those around you. Develop your skills by attending seminars, reading books, and so forth. You'll be astonished at how much you change over time, and you'll have landed some well-paying jobs!

Many professionals want to generate more money as they transition from one position to the next. Obtaining well-paying work can help you achieve significant financial security and achieve your goals. It can be challenging to find well-paying work, so knowing what you can do to enhance your chances is essential. In this piece, we will define a high-paying job, outline how to get one, explain if these positions require a degree, and look at other factors that affect how much you can earn.

Chapter 2

Getting a side hustle

24 Side Jobs That Earn Extra Money

Almost everyone could use a little extra money, but having a full-time job and saving additional money is sometimes enough. Effective side enterprises generate regular revenue streams, vital for making extra money.

People who operate as side hustlers come from many walks of life and sell various commodities. They are resourceful and experimental and perceive resource constraints as an exciting challenge rather than a reason to give up.

If you want to earn extra money, here are some ideas for side jobs:

1. Participate in paid Internet surveys

Many firms and market research organizations want to know what customers think about their products and services. You may earn money by taking surveys on websites like Branded Surveys, Swagbucks, and Survey Junkie. Although taking surveys is unlikely to pay your bills, it can provide you with extra money for the weekend.

2. Make money by reviewing apps and websites.

Nothing stops business faster than a faulty website or an inoperable app. As a result, before something goes live, developers request that testers test it by clicking all the links and interacting with all the buttons.

You may make money doing that. What exactly is this?

A few matchmaking websites that can help you locate many website and app testing jobs are UserTesting, UTest, Userlytics, UserCrowd, and Enroll. Some competitive professions even pay $100 for a 60-minute test to make money here.

3. Transcribe phone conversations, videos, and other audio recordings.

Transcribers receive audio files from their clients and use a computer to capture what they hear. These data may involve films, audio notes, phone calls, or legal processes. Thus a good ear and quick hands are required. For paid transcription opportunities, look into freelancing websites like Rev, TranscribeMe, and GoTranscript.

4. Become a ride-sharing driver.

Individuals interested in driving for a rideshare company nowadays have numerous options. Independent options, such as ZIRO, primarily based in San Francisco, or Wingz, which concentrates on transporting passengers to and from airports and driving for well-known corporations like Uber or Lyft, cater to specific needs or locations.

5. Carry groceries

If you want to drive, you can sign up for grocery delivery apps, but you don't necessarily appreciate having strangers in your car.

Check out Instacart or Spark Driver (Walmart's delivery app) if you're looking for side gigs delivering groceries.

6. Allow visitors to stay at your home.

Renting out your property or extra room might generate a lot of money. Why not make extra money from your home, which you most likely already spend time cleaning and caring for? Airbnb is the most popular platform for renting out properties, but you may also use Vrbo, Agoda, or Plum Guide (UK only).As a supplement, 7. Make food available

Food delivery, like grocery delivery, has become popular in recent years.

With so many apps where you may join up to be a driver, such as UberEats, DoorDash, Grubhub, and Postmates,

8. Begin marketing affiliate products.

Affiliate marketing is promoting someone else's goods or services on your website in exchange for a percentage of any purchases generated from your recommendations. (Typically, via a unique link or code). This is an excellent way to combine side enterprises. If you have a podcast or an online business, consider getting into affiliate marketing. It's a perfect way to produce passive income while pursuing your interests or another side company.

Locate the perfect products on an affiliate marketplace such as Leadpages, ConvertKit, ClickBank, or ShareASale. And if you work as a content creator, course instructor, or e-commerce influencer, the Shopify Affiliate Program could be a great side hustle.

9. Online instructor

Teaching is one of the most rewarding jobs, and because of sites like Cambly, TutorOcean, Preply, and Learn to Be, anyone can tutor kids online. Several young entrepreneurs start freelancing while still in school. The market for test preparation is expected to grow at a 6% annual rate through 2027, owing to the popularity of services such as tutoring and exam preparation among college student freelancers.

10. Dog walking and pet sitting

People nowadays see their pets as family members, so there is a growing demand for trustworthy persons to care for their furry family members.

Finding customers used to be the most challenging part of working as a dog walker or pet sitter, but with apps like Rover, Wag!, PetSitter.com, and PetBacker, it's a lot easier.

11. Set up a Substack blog.

Although monetization is challenging, blogging has long been a popular side hustle. Substack, a platform that allows freelance authors to distribute their work directly to their audience and earn money through recurring subscriptions, is gaining popularity among bloggers.

As a result, bloggers may steadily increase their following and generate a stable monthly income without relying on intrusive advertising, sponsorships, or freelance writing employment.

12. Distribute parcels

Amazon Flex allows you to earn extra money in your spare time. Anyone with the time and a vehicle can now sign up to deliver products through Amazon Flex. Delivery schedules vary; drivers sign up for a block of time and are assigned as many or as few deliveries as possible.

13. Promote your photographs

Many companies, such as Burst, Shutterstock, and Getty Photographs, are continuously looking for photographs to buy for commercials and websites.

New images will always be required because websites must constantly update and revise their information as long as the internet exists.

Obtaining high-quality prints of your photographs is straightforward and inexpensive, so if you have a good idea, there will be a market for it. Print your photos on tangible materials so that you can sell them as wearable and framed art. You may also sell prints of your images or print them on goods such as mugs and sweatshirts. You could charge for your photography skills. Even without considering additional events such as concerts, graduations, pregnancy announcements, yearly family photographs, and so on, photographing weddings may be a full-time career.

14. Begin a podcast

Podcasting, like social media and blogging, has become a pillar of the online content landscape. The popularity of podcasts has grown year after year since their inception.

Furthermore, podcasting is inexpensive. For less than $100, you can acquire an excellent USB microphone (many of which are designed specifically for podcasting), and recording software such as Audacity is free and straightforward.

15. Create and sell your T-shirts.

Assume you like the design and want to get your feet wet in the business world by starting a low-risk print-on-demand business. Shopify apps like Printful, Printify, and Gelato make it simple to put bespoke designs onto t-shirts that are printed and distributed at the point of purchase, eliminating the need to make large inventory purchases upfront.

Clean cars

Most people understand how to wash cars from the inside out, but only a few are eager to do it themselves. That is why it is such a lucrative side hustle. Only a few cleaning supplies are required, some of which you may already have. Many brief car-washing jobs are available in cities worldwide on applications like TaskRabbit, Steady, and Jobble.

17. Increase your income by creating a social media page and using sponsorships.
The term "influencer" is frequently associated with someone who has given up all privacy in return for a devoted following.
You don't have to make yourself the center of attention to be a powerful influencer. Managing social media is a terrific side business idea with much room for innovation. Any web content, including memes, photography, digital art, and even specialist content such as ASMR movies, can be profitable if you can build a dedicated customer base.

18. Go on a neighborhood tour

The advent of platforms like Showaround and Airbnb's Experiences section demonstrates the necessity for a reliable local tour guide.

19. Create homemade items and sell them.

If you've ever wanted to earn money from your hobbies, making and selling homemade items is a terrific side hustle. Even if it takes time to learn a profession, manufacturing handmade goods is one of the best ways to stand out in a sea of mass-produced goods. Consider a task you enjoy even if no one pays you for it. Carpentry, knitting, painting, and other artistic interests can be the foundation for profitable side companies.

20. Mow the grass and do other landscaping tasks

Getting customers. Are simple to incorporate into your spare time.

Launch a dropshipping business.

If you appreciate the mechanical aspects of print-on-demand but are more interested in marketing and operations than in creating distinctive designs, consider starting a drop shipping business.

Drop shipping is another online business technique in which a third party makes and ships your existing products. You only need to set up your store, set your product prices, and market your business.

You can drop ship on internet stores like Amazon and eBay to reach more buyers. There is plenty of space for profit as long as your marketing costs are reasonable. Dropshipping is also a low-risk business because things are only dispatched once purchased.

22. Create a clothing brand

Curating your apparel line is easier than it sounds, especially if you use a dropshipping business model. Starting a clothing business may appear to be a full-time profession rather than a side hustle.

Given the availability of dropshipping clothes providers, most of your work would consist of establishing a following and finding things that will appeal to them.

23. Launch a YouTube channel

Almost two billion people visit YouTube daily and view 250 million hours of video. It takes a long time to build a large enough YouTube following to generate money from commercials, so finding a more immediate revenue stream is better than waiting for ads to become viable. Fortunately, there are several ways to monetize YouTube other than sponsored advertisements.

24. Sell digital goods

Musicians are always in demand for films and commercials. A digital product is any non-physical asset in the digital realm.

MP3s, PDFs, videos, and templates are all examples of products that may be downloaded or streamed.

Websites continuously seek new typefaces and images to differentiate themselves from the competition. Textbooks, royalty-free audio files (such as stock music or sound effects), templates, and other digital goods are examples of digital goods.

Questions to Consider When Starting a Side Business

A side hustle is a great way to supplement your income, but it takes time to establish traction, just like any new business. If you don't choose an idea that fits your lifestyle, it's easy for this extra work to fall to the bottom of your to-do list and be forgotten.

As a result, fascinating side occupations usually feel like a creative outlet that balances craft and commerce rather than a chore. Even while side hustles do not always lead to full-time jobs, many people pursuing them do so after their business thrives.

Here are some things to consider if you want a side business that could eventually lead to your career.

1. Does the plan work with your current schedule?
Because you will devote significant time to this side hustle, it is preferable if it fits within your schedule.
A side business idea should be something you can do in addition to your regular 9 to 5 job that will not conflict with or hinder you from accomplishing it. There will be problems at your full-time job. You may need to work longer hours on some days to complete a project or meet commitments such as meetings and team-building activities.

Working 40 hours a week is enough to deplete most people's creative energy by the end of the day, and after spending quality time with friends and family, finding time for a side business can be challenging.

Side jobs like dog walking, real estate, or babysitting may appear intriguing, but fitting in around your regular day job may be more challenging.

2. Does the concept correspond to your passions and interests?

However, the best time to work hard to launch something is during these tucked-away hours in life's margins. You've watched every true-crime documentary on Netflix, the workday is done, the weekend is still a few days away, and your calendar is clear.

Nonetheless, there may be times when you do not want to work. As a result, even if the end product isn't something you're enthusiastic about, it's ideal if your side business is closely related to it. That could imply that you enjoy some aspect of managing things behind the scenes, learning about a new subject or area of interest, or wanting to help others. Whatever the appeal, a good litmus test is being drawn to the task while you should be doing something else. A little amount of enthusiasm may go a long way.

3. Is it possible to make the idea profitable?
Even if not every passion should be limited by the need for profit, most of us have expenditures and student loans to pay. A good side business, by our criteria, should yield a return on time spent. This means that your side business must be financially and financially secure in the long run; it cannot simply be a part-time side job.
Most side projects fail since your significant responsibilities are enhancing your product or service and determining how to attract your first consumers.
 -profitable. Your business is only suitable if your profit margins or hourly compensation are positive.

Choosing the best part-time employment for you

An underappreciated benefit of side employment is their capacity to serve as a learning environment where you can practice producing good money online. You may rehearse publicly by side hustling and testing your small business ideas. Because most of us rely on regular jobs to make ends meet, creating extra money online necessitates a skill that is not often intuitive.

Furthermore, side employment is more than just a method to supplement your income. Starting a side business allows you to gain valuable skills and improve professionally and as an entrepreneur. A side gig can provide artistic independence and professional progress for writers, actors, painters, musicians, and other artists.

Chapter 3

Get rid of your debts

How to Get Out of Debt in 8 Easy Steps

Carrying too much debt can lead to financial difficulties in various ways. Your ability to obtain more loans, such as mortgages or auto loans, may be impeded if you need help making payments or your credit score falls.

If you have significant debt, you can take numerous steps to get out of debt and back on track financially.

High debt levels may result in low credit ratings, making it more difficult to get financial products.

Consider paying off your lowest debt or credit cards with the highest interest rates first.

Consider cost-cutting measures and apply the money you save to your debt.

Loan forgiveness and income-based repayment programs can help with educational debt. Consult a skilled credit counselor about your options based on your specific situation.

Ways to Get Out of Debt

Debt includes mortgages, student loans, credit card debt, and other types of personal debt. It might be upsetting to be too indebted. Debt relief may improve your financial status and provide you with more possibilities.

1. Accept your debt

Examine your loan statements and bills to ensure that you fully understand how much you owe on each obligation each month and the interest rate you're paying. Make sure that your monthly loan payments and essential expenses surpass your income. If you cannot pay your mandatory fees, you must take action, such as negotiating with lenders or finding more revenue.

2. Create a Repayment Strategy

Decide which debt you want to repay before adding extra money to your commitments. Adopting the avalanche technique to attack high-interest debt first will save you the most money. Others, however, discover that beginning with the smallest debt first keeps them focused and works better for them.

3. Identify the credit history.

Check your credit report for inaccuracies and your credit score. You have the right to see your credit report at least once a year. AnnualCreditReport.com or each credit bureau, Experian, Equifax, and TransUnion, can provide you with one.

Consult your credit report to discover more about the consequences of debt on your credit score.

You can check to see whether you have a lot of late payments or a high credit utilization percentage, which suggests that you are utilizing a lot of your available credit.

4. Make debt adjustments

If your credit allows it, try to secure a more significant, lower-interest loan and combine your responsibilities. You can pay off your loan sooner if you reduce the interest rate. Use one of your credit cards' 0% APR debt transfer deals. Depending on the arrangement, this allows you to take advantage of a grace period between six and 18 months.

If you partially pay off the debt before the promotional time expires, you will be charged the interest rate of the credit card. If you own a home with equity, you can use a home equity line of credit (HELOC) to pay off higher-interest debt. Lines of credit have far lower interest rates than credit cards.

5. Increase your payments by five percent.

Pay off your debt as soon as possible, especially if it has a high-interest rate. Paying more than the minimum required payment may speed up the debt repayment.
If you increase your payment amount, your loan will be paid off sooner and with less interest.

6. Reduce your expenses
Reduced unnecessary expenditure is an essential part of debt relief. Examine your typical spending and determine what is necessary, such as food, shelter, and utilities, and what is not, such as entertainment or clothing. You may have extra income after reducing unnecessary spending that you can use to pay down your debt. Don't cancel your credit cards. Closing credit cards may lower your credit score because it reduces the total amount of credit available and boosts your credit usage ratio.7. Consult an experienced financial advisor.

Speaking with a credit counselor or financial advisor may help you understand your debt-reduction options. Qualified specialists can discuss the best strategies for your specific situation. A credit counselor can assist you when speaking with your creditors. However, be wary of credit professionals who charge exorbitant fees.

8. Consult with lenders about terms.
Consider taking on different activities if you are still struggling to pay off your debt with your salary. If you need to catch up on your payments, try debt sentiment. Your contract with your creditors to pay off a portion of your debt in exchange for a decrease in the overall amount you owe using this strategy. One disadvantage of debt settlement is that it negatively influences your credit score long-term.

There are twenty-eight debt-reduction strategies.

1. Make a budget!

This one is on Jimmy's list since it is so important. The truth is that you can only get out of debt by creating a budget. Period.

Budgeting, on the other hand, does not have to be a chore. Make the process easier by using budgeting software like EveryDollar. A zero-based budget is the most excellent way to give every dollar you earn a purpose, whether for giving, saving, or spending. Your budget will show you where your money is going and, more importantly, where you may save money to add to your debt snowball.

2. Start a secondary hustle.

Starting your own business has always been difficult! You can sell your items on the internet. Do you have a knack for making things?

Do you have a soft spot for animals? Think about dog walking or pet sitting. Learn how to start a side business. You could be surprised at your level of success.

3. Get a part-time job.
You must be interested in starting your own business. Then look into these simple ways to boost your income. Learn how to drive for Lyft or Uber. Alternatively, you may deliver pizzas at night to supplement your income. Working with firms like Uber Eats or Grubhub in your spare time allows you to provide many types of meals. That extra cash each month can help you pay off your debt faster, allowing you to start celebrating sooner!

4. Remove the car!
The average monthly cost of a new car is $667.1. That is absurd! Instead of tossing that $667 auto payment out the window, use it to your debt snowball. Consider how much faster you could get out of debt if you replaced your new, shiny toy in your garage with an old, paid-for vehicle.

5. Throw away your credit cards.

They should be shredded. Remove them. Fire them up. You will never be able to get out of debt unless you quit living in debt.

The credit card industry will try to persuade you that canceling your credit card is a bad idea. Please pay attention: these are incorrect. No matter how many you have, credit cards keep you caught in a debt cycle. Please remove them all and never look back!

6. Employ the envelope system.

You can feel the money leave your hands when you pay with cash. Ouch! People prefer to spend less when paying with cash.

When you utilize your personalized envelope system, you'll see (and feel) every dollar you pay from your envelopes, which will help you keep track of your spending and stick to your budget.

7. Terminate your investments.

Yes, you read that right. Yes, it would be beneficial if you stopped contributing to your 401(k). You want your profits to go toward your debt-reduction approach right now. You can resume retirement savings when you've paid off your obligations and saved 3-6 months' expenditures in a fully funded emergency fund. By then, you'll have completed Baby Step 4 and can begin investing 15% of your income for retirement. Stop comparing yourself to others.

Who came out on top in the comparison game? No. One. Stop attempting to outrun John! Remember, you're living like no one else right now to live and give like no one else hereafter.

Take a look at this. In 20 years, you will have no financial worries, whereas everyone else will still have vehicle loans, mortgages, and credit card bills.

9. Inform the kids that you are on a budget.
Your children can be the wrong source of advice when it comes to money. Bring them on board instead of making them an enemy

of your financial goals! Teach children about money so they understand what you do and what you need additional budget space for. Talk to them about your ambition to be debt-free. And never be afraid to utter the word "no."

10. Attend Financial Peace University.
Financial Peace University (FPU) will educate you on how to get out of debt and save more money step by step. The nine-lesson course can be completed separately or as part of a class for additional accountability. In any case, start FPU today and learn how to get out of debt for good.

11. Take out the coupons.
You've probably heard it a thousand times, but are you doing it? Simply displaying a coupon to the cashier can save you significant money. Just be sure you're using coupons on items you intend to buy; otherwise, you may overspend on things you don't need.

12. Think about going consignment shopping. Children grow out of their clothes at the speed of light. And going into debt to pay for your two-year-old's ever-changing wardrobe isn't worth it. Look for consignment stores that sell gently used clothing in your neighborhood. If you prefer to shop online, thredUP and Swap.com are great venues to locate adult and children's clothing at a fraction of the price.

13. Unplug the cable.
If you enjoy watching TV and saving money, you have options. You can cut the cord by studying the best streaming options for your budget. Put $100 of your monthly cable bill toward your debt and see how quickly it climbs.

14. Stop dining out.
We comprehend. Going out to eat or using the drive-thru is significantly more convenient than making meals at home;

however, while you enjoy the convenience of not cooking for picky eaters, eating out is far more expensive than eating at home.

15. Plan your meals.

So, if restaurants are out of the question, how can you achieve "meals at home" without stress? Begin thinking about food! You will spend less money on food every month. That means you can put more of your hard-earned cash toward debt repayment.

16. Say goodbye to your barista.

Make your coffee. It's a minor modification to your morning routine that will immediately add to your savings. We're convinced that your favorite coffee shop can assist you in figuring out where your money goes each month.

17. Visit the library.

Libraries have existed for quite some time, but guess what? They're still amazing! Any book, e-book, or audiobook can be borrowed for free. The internet has also boosted the value of libraries. The library applications Libby, Hoopla, and Project Gutenberg allow you to find, reserve, and check out books without leaving your couch!

18. Make a grocery list.
Want to know one of the simplest ways to save money at the grocery store? Make a detailed list of everything. Whether you like to make a paper grocery list or use a grocery lists app like Mealime or AnyList, don't walk through those automatic doors without a strategy.

19. Consider buying groceries online.
Of course, convenience comes to mind when weighing the benefits of online vs. in-store grocery shopping. But do you know what else is a huge advantage? Less money spent! In addition to the "online only" savings and other advantages, you can review your shopping cart before pressing "buy now."

That indicates you can overcome such desires.

20. Avoid expensive hobbies.

Do you have $200 per month to spend on golf? Designer fabric for that craft project you've started and abandoned several times? Alternatively, you may add some vintage wine bottles to your collection. Put those costly pleasures on hold for a while—your favorite craft store will still be there when you're debt-free.

21. Resign from your gym membership.

We've heard you can still go outside for a free run. Begin a jogging club with a group of pals. Or try those fancy HIIT workouts at your local park. You can get in shape and stay healthy without breaking the budget. Just be sure you save money on the protein powder you'll never use. Instead, put the money toward your debt-free goal to be debt-free as soon as feasible.

22. Seek free entertainment.

Put a stop to your entertainment spending for the time being. This includes no outings to the movies, concerts, mini-golf, or anything else that is costly. There are less expensive ways to pamper oneself than paying to see an artist perform live. Instead, make it a priority to discover free activities to keep oneself occupied. Instead, look for a free event in your region. Take the kids to the park.

23. Ask for a raise.

Learn how to ask for a raise properly, then put on a confident face and march into your boss's office.

24. Understand the art of saying no.

Learning to say no to buying things you don't need is one of the most creative methods to stop paying for your past and start building your future. Make it a new word in your lexicon. It's incredible. Accept it since you'll have to do it again when you spend money. Most inventive

25. Sell items on Facebook Marketplace or Craigslist.
Have you heard yet? Someone else's trash is someone else's treasure. Examine your kids' bedrooms. Then go through your closet and see if you can get rid of anything. Hold a garage sale if you prefer to sell your items the old-fashioned way.

26. Put a spending freeze in place.
Consider a no-spend day or a "nothing but the essentials" month, sometimes known as a spending freeze. This is a fantastic approach to save some extra money towards that month's debt reduction goal.

27. Provide more information.
Wait a minute—give? Yes! Giving changes you. It transforms your soul and temporarily diverts your attention away from yourself.

Make tithing and sharing a part of your budget, regardless of your income.

28. Create accountability.
It isn't easy to keep to a debt-reduction plan. When you have to decline social invites, concerts, and dining out, it is vital to locate someone you can rely on to hold you accountable for your goals. If you're married, this is your spouse. Your accountability partner could be a close friend or a neighbor. Just make sure it's someone who will point out any mistakes you make. When Learning How to Get Out of Debt, Avoiding Traps
Now that you've learned how to start your debt snowball let's talk about some potential stumbling blocks. Here are a few mistakes to avoid on your path to debt freedom:

1. Debt Consolidation
You've probably heard of it. Maybe you've given in to it. But take it from us: debt consolidation is a bad idea. Consolidating

your loans to get a lower interest rate will give you the impression that you've done anything to improve your circumstances. In practice, however, it will keep you in debt for a more extended period because debt consolidation typically includes a longer repayment period. We can only help with student loan debt consolidation. And only if you consolidate your student loans properly.

2. Credit Card Balance Transfers

Credit card balance transfers, like debt consolidation, are only a short-term fix. Sure, it will provide you with a little more breathing room in your paycheck, but it will keep you in debt for longer.

Why? Because you'll be tempted to spend your "extra" money on things other than debt repayment. Remember that the only way to get out of debt quickly is to give it everything you've got—until it's gone.

3. Filing for Bankruptcy

It isn't good when you need more money to pay your electric bill or buy groceries. However, bankruptcy is rarely a viable option. Take a deep breath and understand there is still hope if you believe bankruptcy is your only alternative. Bankruptcy should be the last resort. Before you leave, make every effort to avoid going there. If you have no other option, please seek the advice of a Ramsey Preferred Coach first. They might give you hope by taking you through various options.

Chapter 4

Living minimalist lifestyle

14 Simple Ways to Improve Your Life Using Minimalism.

If you've ever been interested in minimalist living, this will help you get started in the right direction. In these simple ways, you can begin to live a minimalistic lifestyle. You will be inspired to become a minimalist in seven distinct ways. What matters most in minimalism is why you own things rather than what you own. When you have less need, you will receive more.

Who wouldn't want less stuff, more significant space, fewer items, and higher quality?

When we glanced around our houses, we used to feel like our stuff owned us. They took up a lot of space in our home.

Why have we accumulated so much stuff? How did we end up outgrowing our 1,200-square-foot house even before we had children? Making my home more minimalistic is always at the top of my priority list when spring or summer approaches. It's about time we planned a weekend to arrange and do a garage sale! Let's talk about minimalist living and reducing your possessions without sacrificing enjoyment.

What Does It Mean to Live Minimally?
A neatly organized kitchen
The phrases "tidy" and "simple" best describe minimalist life. In other words, make positive improvements to the simplicity of your existence.
Consider a home with clean, uncluttered rooms (no clutter hidden beneath beds or on top of closet shelves), bookshelves with enough space to read the books, open areas

with sparkling worktops, and cheerful people all about.

Why? As a result, you spend less time focusing on your belongings and more time doing things you enjoy, such as spending time with family or participating in hobbies. This is the basic concept of the minimalist living movement. The minimalist and frugal lifestyles share many similarities. Both embody the idea that living well on a limited budget is feasible, yet they differ in some ways.

Although maintaining a minimalist lifestyle may result in less money spent over time because you buy fewer "things," this is not usually the goal.

The goals are to be clutter-free and to live; simplifying everyday life at home is more essential than saving money. A person who lives a frugal lifestyle will save money because they buy less "stuff," but the items they believe may have lower sticker costs than an identical item purchased by a minimalist.

Why Should You Live a Minimalist Lifestyle? Some people connect minimalism with living. However, this is different! You remove clutter and belongings you rarely use or need to spend less time cleaning and experience less stress in your home. A minimalist lifestyle has numerous advantages, not the least of which is saving money and having less to clean! As a result, these two lifestyles might significantly overlap while yet diverging.

Who wouldn't want to clean faster?
Additional benefits may include the following:
More time available
Feeling more relaxed and less stressed
Make an effort to be more ecologically sensitive.

Reduce your money difficulties.

Improve your relationships with family and friends. If you want to learn everything there is to know about minimalism, the finest minimalist websites, such as The Minimalists and Becoming Minimalist, are excellent places to start.

Where Do I Begin Living a Minimalist Life?

There's no need to go overboard when you start—avoid getting rid of anything and everything! Owning less entails more than simply throwing everything away at first!

Remember, the most straightforward technique is to search a room for anything you classify as "trash" or "merely taking up space."

Look for those things that irritate you 90% of the time, even if you have no idea why! Mainly if you use them sparingly. You've probably heard the expression "use it or lose it." Be bold when saying your goodbyes!

So, whether at the recycling center or the trash can, you need certain goods to find new homes.

Where Do I Begin Living a Minimalist Life?
You've probably heard the expression "use it or lose it." Be bold when saying your goodbyes! So, whether at the recycling center or the trash can, you need certain goods to find new homes. You may also consider the benefits and drawbacks of various aspects of your lifestyle.

Consider cutting back. Is your home far more significant than you and your family will ever require? Is it a bright idea for a single person or a young couple to buy a house? Examine Airbnb's home-sharing alternatives.

Is the first house you're considering big enough for the number of people you plan to have as a family? Knowing there is a risk of too much space, you will be motivated to fill up. It may be wiser for your situation to purchase a larger "forever home" and skip the starter home phase. However, if you had fewer items, you may

Do the "things" in your house constantly make you feel like a slave? Endless laundry, weekly housekeeping that includes dusting a billion trinkets, and so on? It might be time to think about organizing a donation drive.
If you can identify even a few areas of your life where simplifying might provide visible benefits, I'd say it's time to dive in and get started.

How to Live Minimally in a Large and Uncluttered Space
There's no reason you can't or shouldn't start making your life look more minimalistic right now! While minimalist living with a family may be a little more complex than living in a single person's or couple's home, this list of tips for where to

start will help ANY family return to a simple life.

Here are some things you can do right now to improve your life.

1. Get rid of collections if you want to live a minimalist lifestyle. Collections are pricey and take up a lot of space. A group of designer handbags will be costly and take up a lot of space. If you can, sell your collection on Amazon or eBay.I have a collection of mugs. I received two more profiles as gifts at the end of the school year. I decided against adding them to my collection. I keep them in a small cupboard next to the coffee machine. My mug collection will eventually be reduced, but I find it tough to part with it.

2. Take advantage of library readers.
Libraries should be more utilized. We may begin by giving away books we've read or selling used textbooks online. There are numerous books on our bookshelf. The

second step is to obtain the books we want to read. Books will swiftly replace other things as your favorite thing if you adopt a minimalist lifestyle.

As a result, we are under pressure to read the books and return them before the deadline. I can't tell you how often I've put down and picked up books.
Because you can't keep track of time.
You'll keep motivated if you have a deadline.

3. Make meal preparation easier.
Right now, I respect this modest approach more than ever! My spice rack and pantry have recently been cleaned. Many items were discarded since they needed to be updated. When I'm trying to prepare gourmet foods, I occasionally buy odd ingredients, even if the recipe calls for a teaspoon, and then they sit in my cabinet for years until they go wrong.

By simplifying meals, the components are simplified. Instead of buying new ingredients, cook using what you already have.

Using a service like the $5 Meal Plan is another good option for simplifying meals.

4. Tidy up your rooms.

If your stuff controls you and takes over your home, it's time to let go.

People have so many goods in their houses that they don't even use, and you can donate the item or sell it on Decluttr, at a garage sale, or on Facebook Marketplace.

I've been going through our house, room by room, in preparation for a garage sale.

Furthermore, we use this time to pack up everything we haven't used in a year in preparation for our local church's summer flea market.

Our closets and the kitchen are the two rooms we've spent the most time arranging. Clothes shrink, pill, and shift throughout the year. After taking a look, adjust your clothes. Is it true that you require many pairs of jeans? The primary issue in our kitchen is the small appliances. Sell it or give it away! It is only needed if you have used it for a year.

Making the most of your space in a small kitchen like ours is critical to its functionality. Consider investing in high-quality items with several uses, such as an instant pot (your meal preparation and planning will thank you). If you want to rent out your extra room to make some extra money on the side, having a decluttered home can help. If someone wants to rent our house on Airbnb, keeping personal stuff to a minimum would be advantageous.

5. Improve your cleaning practices and keep your home office basic.

In addition to decluttering, pushing yourself to keep flat surfaces as clean as possible would be beneficial. That indicates that your home desk consists solely of your computer and a cup to store a few pencils.

How may this help you live a simpler life?
If you can't store something on a flat table out in the open, you'll have to find a "home" for it. You know you have too much stuff when you need more storage space!
When not in use, ensure that everything is always in its proper "home," or at the very least, do a once-daily pick-up and return everything.

Laundry should be put in a hamper (or washed!), dishes should be rinsed, and mail should be sorted and filed as soon as it enters the house rather than piling up on the desk or counters until it is cleaned and put away.

6. Move quickly
I need to change my behavior as I migrate to a simple existence. Traveling light is difficult

for me. When I travel, I like to be organized and have options.

Many people may need help with this. I've learned a few travel tips that have helped me pack lighter.

My particular favorite has been the TSA-approved reusable travel bottles. These are ideal for Caribbean holidays or weekend camping trips.

7. Say no!

I'm not afraid to say no. How my post on saying no will affect living a simple lifestyle? Simple! My in-laws inquired if we needed a lot of stuff they were getting rid of when they moved. We avoided clutter in our home by refusing to accept it. One thing you can deny is a larger house. When preparing to buy your first home, avoid making mistakes because having a larger home is troublesome on many levels!

Purchasing a more prominent home may make life more difficult. Instead of being content with less, you may be tempted to fill the empty places in your home.

You spend more money on more rooms, many of which you may never use! Many people consider it a waste of money.
Having a large monthly mortgage payment might put a burden on your budget. Furthermore, the cost of ownership, upkeep, taxes, and so on rises with the size of the house.

Why buy a bigger house than you need? Life is worth living because of our experiences and memories! The second issue is that it allows more "things" to be filled while taking up more space. You will need additional furniture and room furnishings. Refuse! The larger your home, the more constrained your life gets.

8. an old pair of black boots were transformed into planters to simplify life.

Learn how to make your products more environmentally friendly. Make novel and innovative uses of household things. Use washable, reusable paperless towels instead of pricey rolls.

We bought the Nest thermostat to lower our carbon footprint while saving money. The Nest learns our breathing patterns and adjusts our heating and cooling systems accordingly. Taking action today will save you money and assist our lovely world for years.

9. Choose multipurpose items over single-purpose items.
When we say something is multipurpose, we think of a couch that transforms into a bed, a multitool, a Swiss Army knife instead of a whole toolbox, or perhaps an outstanding old spork. I'll use makeup as an example because many of us have favorites and a cache of extras we never use.

What about you? Are you one of the women who only own one item of lipstick, eyeliner, eye shadow, blush, bronzer, concealer, foundation, and brows?

That's eight pieces, and most girls probably don't just have one eye shadow! I've recently discovered several items, such as eyeliner and brow pencils, concealer and highlighter, and blush and eyeshadow. Isn't it better to streamline your spending, routine, and storage?

10. Cut back on spending to make fewer purchases.

Allowing yourself room to spend in your clothing, miscellaneous, eating out, or "fun" budget categories when you work on your monthly budget will make it much easier to spend more money than necessary.

Give yourself less wiggle room in these categories (and actively work on actively shrinking it month to month). You'll find yourself with much more money to do better things with, such as investing for retirement, saving for an emergency fund, or even putting towards your next big purchase to avoid taking on more debts.

Less impulsive purchases benefit both your wallet and your living space!

11. When it makes sense, buy in quantity.
Bulk shopping can be a great way to live a minimalist lifestyle while streamlining your meals. You must do it correctly if you hoard everything just because it's on sale, a good deal, or whatever. If you seldom serve spaghetti as a side dish and instead prefer potatoes or rice, buying 20 pounds of those when they're on sale makes a lot of sense. Win-win! Granted, you'll have more to store than you need right now, but you'll save money and use the room for something you'll use in the long term.

12. Avoid spending money unless necessary.
On a lesser income, minimalism is undoubtedly harsh; you may have little money left each month for savings. This is

why, regardless of your circumstances, it is critical to live a more modest lifestyle, keep your promises, and work hard to attain financial independence.

You may save money for your mental health and your desired extraordinary experiences.

This is where minimalism's economical (and thrifty) side comes into play because it places a high emphasis on experiences and a low value on commodities.

If you stay focused and "keep your eyes on the prize," you may be able to live a modest but enjoyable lifestyle.

Mint and Empower (previously Personal Capital) are two online budgeting apps that simplify analyzing your expenditure and finding areas where you may save money.

13. Make money management easy.

Get ready to write a check to pay a bill.

Even if basic living is mainly about the stuff in your life, you should always remember the one thing that keeps the globe turning!

Although a minimalist lifestyle does not always emphasize saving money and minimizing spending, adjusting your routines to live more frugally may be an excellent habit to develop.

When paying off debt, you should use a more planned strategy, such as basic budget templates.

Maintain accounts for retirement, emergency savings, and so on if needed. Try using one savings account (separate from your emergency fund) and tracking your savings progress using a simple spreadsheet.

Or a budgeting program like Empower.

The same is valid for checking accounts. Many people believe that having separate checking accounts for "fun money," flexible spending (such as groceries or clothing), and utilities/fixed obligations is applicable. This is an excellent method for forgetting how much money you have and what you do with it (in addition to the numerous savings accounts).

Among the ways to reduce your expenses are:
Limit yourself to one card if you must use credit cards (and can avoid falling victim to their various traps). You can maintain greater control over your expenditures if you do not divide your expenses among numerous somewhat disguised sources.
Get out of debt as quickly as possible if you haven't already!
Reduce recurring costs wherever possible (how many streaming services do you require?).

14. Be grateful

By possessing less and living with less, you can become more grateful and appreciative of what you have in your life. This is the last advice since it is not the least important or practical. Even still, it is the most difficult for many people to execute, not just those who desire to live a minimalist lifestyle. We always forget how much we DO have to be thankful for, no matter how bad the rest of our lives appear at the time.

If you're continuously wishing you had something, you're setting yourself up to want to surround yourself with "stuff." You're ruining all your hard work to get rid of items you don't need and creating a habit of using and appreciating what you have.

Even if you want a more excellent/newer car, a cleaner home, or a higher paycheck, take the time to appreciate what you have. This puts you in a better frame to truly appreciate things when they improve.

Chapter 5

Start investing for confortable life

14 Fantastic Ways to Invest Small Sums

7 Steps to a Successful Investing Adventure

The greatest successful investors only emerged after some time. It takes time and patience, not to mention trial and error, to learn the ins and outs of the financial world and your personality as an investor. This article will walk you through the first seven steps of your investing journey and show you what to look for.

Your investment journey begins with a plan and a time frame; once you know how long you intend to invest and what you hope to gain, you can put the framework in place to reach your goals.

Next, educate yourself on how the market works, what investment plan is ideal for you, and what type of investor you are.

Be cautious of who you seek guidance from, and be aware of your preconceptions and assumptions as you seek the best path for yourself. Ensure you understand this is a long-term journey, so short-term disappointments don't throw you off; always keep an open mind and learn from your mistakes.

1. How to Begin Investing

Successful investment is a journey, not a one-time event, and you must prepare as if you were embarking on a long trip. Begin by deciding where you want to go, then organize your investment trip accordingly. For example, do you want to retire at 55 in 20 years?

How much money will you require to do this task? It would be preferable if you asked these questions first. Your investment objectives will determine the plan you develop.

2. Understand what works in the market.
Read literature on modern financial concepts or enroll in an investment course. For a good reason, the Nobel Prizes were awarded to those who developed theories such as portfolio optimization, diversification, and market efficiency—investing syntheses science (financial basics) and art (qualitative variables). Finance's scientific side is an excellent place to start and should be addressed. Don't worry if science isn't your strong suit. Many texts, including Stocks

After you know what works in the market, you may develop simple principles that work for you.

Are you an individualist, an explorer, a guardian, or a superstar when it comes to investing?

3. Understand Your Investment Strategy
Nobody understands you or your position better than you. As a result, you may be the most competent person to invest—all you need is a little assistance. Fund managers created a useful behavioral model that assists investors in understanding themselves. Identify and manage the personality qualities that will help or hinder your ability to support successfully.

Strategy for Investment
The model categorizes investors based on two personality traits: manner of action (careful or reckless) and level of confidence (confident or apprehensive).
 The strategic model separates investors into five groups based on these personality traits:

Individualists are cautious and self-assured, and they frequently do things themselves.
Volatile, entrepreneurial, and determined adventurer

Celebrity - someone who follows the latest investment trends

The Guardian is a highly risk-averse, wealth-preserving individual.
Straight Arrow - possesses all of the above properties in equal measure. Individualists with analytical behavior, confidence, and a keen eye for value have the highest investing returns. If you discover that your personality attributes are similar to those of an adventurer, you can still achieve investment success if you alter your plan accordingly. In other words, no matter which group you belong to, you must manage your core assets in a systematic and disciplined manner.

4. Know Your Enemies and Friends
Be wary of phony allies who claim to be on your side, such as unethical investment advisors whose interests may conflict with yours. It would help if you also kept in mind that, as an investor, you are competing with

larger financial institutions with faster access to information.; more resources, significantly more significance, and quicker access to information.

Keep in mind that you may be your own worst adversary. You may be undermining your success based on your personality, strategy, and specific circumstances. If a guardian followed the latest market trend and sought short-term rewards, they would act against their personality type. Because you are risk-averse and value wealth preservation, substantial losses as a result of

High-risk, high-return investments would have a significantly more significant impact on you. Be honest with yourself, and identify and adjust the elements stopping you from successfully investing or moving you out of your comfort zone.

5. Determine the Best Investment Strategy

Your level of education, personality, and resources should determine your direction. Investors typically employ one of the following strategies:

Put only some of your eggs in a single basket. In other words, broaden your horizons.
Please put all your eggs in one basket, but keep an eye on it. Most successful investors begin with diversified low-risk portfolios and gradually learn by doing. Investors who obtain superior knowledge through time are better prepared to take a more active role in their portfolios. Make tactical bets on a core passive portfolio to combine these techniques.

6. Commit to the Long Term
The best long-term approach might not be the most exciting investing option. However, your chances of success should improve if you stick with it and don't let

your emotions or "false friends" get the better of you.

7. Be Open to Learning
The market is challenging to forecast, but one thing is sure: it will be tumultuous.
. Learning to be a good investor takes time, and the investment journey is often lengthy. The market will occasionally prove you wrong. Recognize this and learn from your mistakes.

1. Automate your investing with Betterment Exchange-traded Funds (ETF) Portfolios.
There are various "robo advisors," online financial services offering skilled portfolio management at meager costs. Betterment is an excellent choice for small investors. First, you must complete an online questionnaire allowing the site to determine your risk tolerance.

Based on that assessment, a portfolio with a diverse allocation of exchange-traded funds

(ETFs) is created for you. When you purchase ETFs, you buy a diversified portfolio of stocks you do not have to manage. Because of this allocation, your only responsibility is to finance your account; you are not responsible for investment selection or rebalancing. Through its Betterment Core, Goldman Sachs Smart Beta, and Innovative Technology portfolios, they presently offer a variety of investing options:

These portfolios give you access to well-known ETFs from Vanguard and iShares, two famous names in the investment world. Betterment Investments does not have a minimum starting account deposit requirement. And in case you didn't notice.

Betterment allows you to start investing with just $0.You can open an account with as little as $100 in monthly donations. The annual maintenance charge on bills under

$100,000 is 0.25% of the account balance. If you aren't ready to invest, they also offer a "No-fee" checking account with a competitive variable rate more significant than your bank (currently 0.35%). The management fee is set on a sliding scale and decreases as your account balance increases.

2. The Balanced Stock Portfolio of M1 Finance

M1 Finance has brought a great new perspective on investing. They, like Betterment, let you invest automatically in various sectors, but the brokerage also enables you to trade stocks and ETFs for free. That's right. It's entirely free! M1 Finance offers by far the most no-fee investments of any brokerage.

M1Finance now lets you purchase fractional stock shares. If Apple stock trades at $400 per share, you may buy $50 and own 12.5%. Finally, before you invest a single dollar, M1 Finance provides a free financial study.

3. Making a $10 Real Estate Portfolio

Fundrise simplifies real estate investing.

You may invest in real estate through this REIT without flipping houses or becoming a landlord. The Fundrise principle is simple: your money is invested in real estate developments. When they make money, you make money.

How much money is involved? Your returns will vary depending on the project you participate in. Still, Fundrise clients earned more than 11% on average last year thanks to technology that discovers excellent real estate projects for you to invest in based on your goals.

Fundrise's most vital feature is the lowest minimum.

If you've ever dabbled in real estate investing, you know it is costly.

Fundrise, on the other hand, permits investors who do not have hundreds of dollars to invest. You can invest as little as $10 with Fundrise. Usually, you'd need $1,000 to invest with them, but their "Starter Portfolio" temporarily allows smaller investors to participate. While Fundrise will invest in the best initiatives for you, you may also get more involved by investing in one of Fundrise's projects.

4. Repayment of Debts

You should pay off your debts for two reasons. The first rule is to avoid investing if you are in debt, especially unsecured debt. The second reason is that paying off debt is the most significant way to ensure an above-average return on investment. This is especially true if the interest rate is double-digit - no guaranteed double-digit profits are available to the average investor.

If you have high-interest debt, you might explore getting a personal loan with a lower interest rate and using the money to pay off the higher-interest debt. Assume you have a $1,000 credit card bill with a 15.99% annual interest rate. Paying down that card secures a roughly 16% rate of return on your money for the rest of your life!

Fiona is a site that analyzes hundreds of lenders' loans, credit cards, savings accounts, and student loan refinancing options. Everything happened in a couple of seconds.

5. Savings Accounts
To be sure, your bank investments will provide little profit.
However, one advantage banks offer is the ability to invest a tiny amount of money in a savings account, receive a small interest, and be risk-free.

Savings accounts are not widely used.
A savings account is best used to save a more significant amount of wealth for future higher-risk/better-reward investments.

Some of the assets on this list will require a minimum commitment of $500 or $1,000. While that is a little money, if you're just getting started with a small investment, your best strategy may be to take your time and save some cash before extending your investment alternatives.

Your Employer-Sponsored Retirement Plan This is the most straightforward method for investing small sums of money, even if you have no money. This is because it is usually set up as a payroll deduction, allowing you to assign a percentage.

Depending on the requirements imposed by the workplace plan, you can assign practically any amount of your salary, ranging from 1% to 20% or more.

You don't even need a large nest egg to invest this way. Put tiny quantities into your account with each paycheck and then begin investing in whatever investments your available funds (and work plan) permit. The most excellent part is the tax breaks! Your contributions are tax-deductible, and the income earned by your assets is tax-free until you retire and begin withdrawing funds.

Furthermore, if your employer matches your contribution, you will receive free money for merely saving a little.

Regardless of how much money you have to invest, investing in your employer-sponsored retirement plan should be one of your first steps.

7. Set up a Roth (or Traditional) IRA.

Start with a Roth IRA or a Traditional IRA.

If your employer does not provide a retirement plan, you can create one independently. All that is required to qualify is earned money. The two best options for most people are a traditional IRA or a Roth IRA.

Similarly to an employer-sponsored retirement plan, any investment gains you earn are tax-deferred until you begin withdrawing the assets in retirement.

Contributions to a traditional IRA are often tax deductible as well.

Contributions to a Roth IRA are not tax deductible; however, withdrawals are tax-free provided you are at least 59 12 at the time of departure and have participated in the plan for at least five years.

And, while there is no employer matching contribution (because there is none), a self-directed traditional or Roth IRA can be maintained in a brokerage account, giving you virtually endless investing alternatives.

You can contribute up to $6,500 to a traditional or Roth IRA each year ($7,500 if you are 50 or older), which means you can build up a significant portfolio in a matter of years.

With the best Roth IRA providers, there is also a meager entry cost. We've presented Three investing choices thus far: Betterment, M1 Finance, and Fundraise. This is excellent news for all of the small investors out there!

8. prosper Prosper functions in the same way as Lending Club does. You can invest as little as $25, which allows you to spread a few hundred dollars among multiple loans. There is also a minimum net worth requirement, which varies by state.

According to Prosper, the average yearly return on a note is 16%, which is a tremendous return for a fixed-rate investment. Prosper, and Lending Club exposes you to the risk of losing your principal if one or more of your loans default. As with bank investments, there is no FDIC to protect your money. Prosperity was also assessed for both borrowers and lenders. There you may learn more about the platform.

9. United States Treasury Securities
You might invest in US Treasury Securities if you want a more conservative investment to protect your principal from market swings. These are debt obligations issued by the United States Treasury Department to fund the national debt. Securities have maturities ranging from 30 days to 30 years (but longer-term maturities may pose a principal risk if sold before maturity).

Using the platform, you can purchase US government assets as low as $100. These securities can be purchased through the US Treasury Department's Treasury Direct program. You can also sell your investments there without incurring any fines.

Treasury Inflation-Protected Securities (TIPS) can also be purchased using Treasury Direct. These pay interest and periodically modify the principal to account for inflation based on changes in the Consumer Price Index.

Investing in Your Skills 10
Are there any talents you could learn that would help you advance in your career? Consider taking a public speaking or sales training course or learning a new computer application or a foreign language. You can learn specific skills to help you advance in your current job or transfer to a new, higher-paying position with another company. A few hundred dollars is typically all required to enroll in a school to learn that skill.

11. Make a Dividend Reinvestment Plan
These programs, often known as DRIPS, allow you to invest small amounts of money in dividend-paying equities. Many large enterprises offer DRIPS, so if you want to invest directly in stocks and prefer certain companies, you can do so - usually without incurring any investment expenses.

DRIPS allows you to gradually increase your investment by making recurring installments. Payroll deductions are commonly utilized to do this.

This is also an excellent method for dollar cost averaging your way into significant investments in major organizations. When you receive dividends, the money is immediately reinvested to buy more company stock.

12. Low Investment Exchange-traded funds (ETFs) and mutual funds

Mutual funds and ETFs have different initial investment minimums. Many require several thousand dollars to start an account, but some allow you to open an account with much less. One example is the Schwab Total Stock Market Index (SWTSX). You could put $1,000 in ten different funds with such a low required minimum.

Check with any significant mutual fund family and numerous investment brokerage firms to see which funds are available with an initial deposit of $1,000 or less. Index funds may be your best bet because they reflect the market's performance.

13. Online Brokerage Firms

Many inexperienced investors are startled to hear they may open an account with an online brokerage firm for $1,000 or less. For example, the minimum initial deposit to open an account with Charles Schwab is $1,000. Still, this amount can be waived if you set up an automatic monthly transfer of $100 via direct deposit or Schwab MoneyLink, or if you open a Schwab Bank High Yield Investor Checking account linked to your brokerage account.

Furthermore, there is no necessary minimum initial deposit to open a brokerage account with TD Ameritrade.

The advantage of investing through a brokerage firm is that you will be presented with a broader selection of investment possibilities than direct investments alone.

14. Your Own Business

So far, I've recommended investing in other businesses, but investing in your firm may be the best alternative if you have a modest amount of money to invest. For example, you can buy a competent lawnmower and start cutting lawns for a few hundred dollars. With just a few hundred dollars, you might have more than $5,000 to invest in no time. After all, who better to invest in than yourself?

You might even develop a website dedicated to selling a particular product range. You may also start a blog and utilize it to negotiate affiliate sales contracts.

If you're interested, you can go to garage sales, estate sales, flea markets, and thrift stores, or you can buy unusual goods and resale them for a profit on eBay or Craigslist.

With technical breakthroughs and the advent of the Internet, starting your own home-based business on a shoestring budget is now easier than ever. Many business owners begin by working a part-time job or doing a side hustle to supplement their income while establishing their firm. Starting your own business may be the most profitable venture if you invest a few hundred dollars.

Becoming an Uber driver is a beautiful side business; you can choose your schedule, sit back, and drive, earning extra money to go toward your dream!

Chapter 6

Positive affirmation for wealth and success

10 Affirmations for Success That Will Change Your LifeWhen utilized appropriately and consistently. Success affirmations can prevent you from thinking negatively and sabotaging your efforts. They can help you re-program your mind and eliminate restrictive notions.

If you envision yourself as someone who can accomplish anything they set their mind to, chances are you will become that person. Achievement is a game of the mind.

Positive affirmations serve as a conduit for communication between the mind's conscious (thinking) and subconscious (activity) sides. Every day, we utilize positive affirmations for success or negative affirmations for failure.

Pessimistic affirmations are often associated with low self-esteem, poor decision-making, and a defeatist mindset. You can use positive affirmations for success, one of the simplest and least expensive ways to improve your mind and well-being, or you can take matters into your own hands and engage in a procedure known as self-hypnosis to calm and regulate your mind.

The Importance of Confident Statements
Many people need help to reach their full potential because they must act to accomplish their dreams and goals. They continue to hold the restricted views their parents or other prominent persons instilled in them.
How to Use Positive Thinking to Your Advantage

You must utilize daily success affirmations to achieve your goals and stay going.

When you use positive affirmations for success, your subconscious mind receives a positive message. Positivity can help you attract more money, better health, and higher status.

10 Motivational Success Phrases
Positive affirmations can assist us in maintaining the proper mindset even in the face of unexpected hurdles. All we have to do is employ the words of knowledge currently available to us to go forward. You can change your life by using these ten affirmations for success:

1. My body and mind are healthy, and my spirit is at peace.
A healthy body is built on a sound mind and soul. Each of these will be affected if one has a bad experience.
You are the leading cause of illness. You are steadily overcoming your illness and winning the war against it through everyday affirmations. Since you understand their

anguish, you can also retract and revoke whatever permission you mistakenly or knowingly provided to everyone or anything in the universe.

2. I am capable of accomplishing anything.
If you want to be in control of your life, you must tell yourself this every day. By saying this, you are giving your mind the sense that you can achieve everything you want.

3. Everything that is happening right now is for my ultimate good.
There are no victims, accidents, or coincidences. They are nonexistent in this reality since you and others only attract what you are a part of.
Recognize in your heart that everything happens in perfect harmony and for a reason.

4. I am the architect of my life; I created the foundation and will pick what goes inside.

Every day is a new beginning that inspires others around you. You can do whatever you want with that day because you are the maker of your own life. To set yourself up for success, practice morning affirmations (positive phrases you tell yourself).

If you begin your day with a powerful affirmation of thought and mood, your day will be changed into something extraordinary. Plan your day and life from the ground up to create something you will like in the long run.

5. I gradually detached myself from persons who have previously hurt me and forgave them.

Forgiveness is being at peace with what someone did and the lessons it taught you rather than forgetting what they did to you.

Your ability to forgive allows you to continue, and how you respond to any occurrence is unaffected by what others think of you.

6. I have limitless potential for accomplishment and unending ability to overcome hurdles.

According to this, your only limitations are those you set on yourself.

What kind of life are you looking for? What is stopping you? What constraints do you impose on yourself?

With the help of this affirmation, you can break through each of those barriers.

7. Today, I abandon my old habits instead of new, beneficial ones.

Recognize that each challenging event is merely a stage in life. As you accept the new, your old behaviors will go away.

You have fully adapted to being a creative being, and this creative energy surges through you, generating new and distinct ideas and the mindset that allows that energy to flow.

8. I have a sense of grandeur.

One of the most effective affirmations for success is to tell yourself daily that you are capable of all excellence in life.

Concentrate on your dreams and visions and connect them to a sensation. By repeating this positive affirmation and believing in your ability to succeed, you empower yourself to create the life you desire.

9. I'm filled with zeal and excitement today.

The source of joy is internal rather than external. It also starts the moment you wake up.

Make it a habit to repeat encouraging statements to yourself first thing in the morning to remind yourself that you can generate positive energy at any moment, regardless of what is happening around you.

Consider yourself to be a stationary lighthouse as the waves pound on it. Its light never moves from its position and absorbs everything around it. Experiment with your thinking in the same way. Keep your happiness near your lighthouse, and don't let the waves disrupt your peace.

10. I accept and love myself.
Self-love is said to be the purest and most ideal form of love. You begin to esteem and respect yourself when you genuinely love yourself. If you are confident and proud of what you accomplish, you will see yourself in a new light and be encouraged and inspired to do more extensive and better things if you use positive affirmations for success.
Have Self-Belief in Your Ability to Create Opportunities
As you repeat these or any other positive affirmations, your brain will begin to work, attracting favorable conditions through the law of attraction while eliminating negative thoughts.

Before you know it, doors will open for you to begin your path toward whatever you wish. If you want more positive affirmation inspiration, try one of these ten uplifting, positive affirmation apps to help you refocus on the go. Positive affirmations will only help you succeed if you act on them. It would be ideal if you were successful. It would help if you kept an open mind and the confidence to act when an opportunity arises.

17 Money affirmations to help you attract financial wealth

It takes time and effort to change or break old habits. While it would be nice to believe that 21 days of practice will change everything (as described in this Forbes article), the truth is that transformation necessitates a consistent approach and dedication over time. This could imply that it takes longer than 21 days.

If you're serious about changing your financial outlook, pick a couple of your favorites from this list and try to put them into practice daily.

Seven abundance affirmations

1. I regard wealth as a crucial component of my existence.
2. I can deal with any financial difficulties that may emerge.
3. I am capable of meeting my financial goals.
4. I've decided to pursue my financial goals today.
5. I wish I had more money. That's perfectly fine.
6. Being wealthy and successful comes easily to me.
7. I live a healthy and prosperous life.
8. Abundance is approaching; I deserve and embrace it.
I accept and receive unexpected funds.
10. I accept and enjoy unexpected prosperity.
I have more money than I require.
12. I have a right to more money.
13. I'm constantly seeking new ways to get money.

14. Money comes to me in unexpected and predictable ways.

15. I am open to receiving whatever fortune life has in store.

16. I'm not poor; I have little wealth right now. That is starting to change.

17. I'm getting out of the way when it comes to money.

Financial Abundance Affirmations
While it is simple to create unfavorable attitudes toward money, those opposing viewpoints typically constrain us to analyze the pattern that perpetuates the situation rather than altering it.

If you've suffered financial losses, find a mantra to help you see them as financial lessons rather than disappointments.

FInancial-abundance-money-affirmation
I am entitled to and expect financial success. I am capable of creating a solid financial basis.

My breadth of experience has played an essential role in my life.

Financial success is okay to me.

I can commercialize my skills.

New money streams will find their way to me.

My financial condition is going to improve.

I am confident in my capacity to make wise financial decisions.

Money Affirmations Money affirmations are beliefs that a specific outcome, such as making a lot of money, is possible. These claims exist as future truths that you hope to attain.

Money attracts me, and I am drawn to it.

Money comes readily and quickly to me.

I am aware of opportunities for earning money.

I understand how to manage money.

I am financially deserving.

My financial situation is becoming better.

Positive Money Mantras + Affirmations

Money mantras should be your biggest supporters. Use them to foster resilience and effect change.

I always have cash.

I'll make money in both expected and unexpected places.

In more ways than one, I am lucky.

My life is whole and wonderful.

My financial goals will be met.

My money helps to make the world a better place. I am entitled to happiness and success.

My money will help both me and those I care about.

We can boost our resilience and self-competence by using money affirmations to reduce emotional spending triggers.

With a Money Abundance Attitude, you can repair your emotional spending.

In today's world, impulsive spending is not uncommon.

You're constantly assaulted with ads, social media with the promise of "keeping up with the Joneses," and the option to shop online with same-day delivery. Jealousy and sorrow are common emotional spending triggers that jeopardize one's self-worth. Don't let destructive emotions influence your money decisions or your financial account.

What Is Emotional Spending, Exactly?
Emotional spending is a type of impulse buying in which you buy something you don't need or, in some situations, want. Emotional spending has no substantial negative implications when done in moderation. However, in extreme cases, this purchase may end in financial difficulties owing to overdraft fees, debt, or bankruptcy.

The following are examples of common impulse spending triggers:
Sadness
Stress

Boredom
Feeling powerless
Jealousy

It might bring me comfort when I manage my money effectively.
I am a frugal spender.
It's fun to spend wisely.
I can save money to move closer to financial independence.
I will not stand in the way of your financially secure life.
I am confident in my capacity to make wise financial decisions.
My spending habits are under my control.
It makes me happy to know that I am spending wisely.

How to Personalize Your Money Affirmations
While current money mantras might be beneficial, creating a personalized affirmation is more tailored to your situation and significantly impacts your

ideas and beliefs. When constructing your mantras, keep the principles of successful claims in mind.

The following should be included in your affirmations:
Be concise.
Concentrate on introspection.
Prepare for a specific conclusion. Make plans for the future.

Aside from daily affirmations, consider the following tried-and-true methods for better money management:

Make Your Financial Plan
Even if you don't have much money right now, a personal finance plan can help you make the most of it. It also motivates you to look into ways to enhance your existing financial prospects, such as saving or realizing how much you spend on Amazon monthly.

Make a Budget

Budgeting does not have to be synonymous with giving up your way of life! Positive thinking and planning can assist you in achieving your objectives without relying on chance or windfall. At their core, budgets can be a fantastic tool for minimizing emotional overspending and keeping track of where your money is going.

Make a Savings Strategy

What better way to promote your financial affirmations job than to increase profits? Selecting a high-yield savings account and establishing weekly and monthly savings goals will allow you to capitalize on life's economic opportunities.

Maintain Your Financial Knowledge

Even if you are a money magnet and constantly receive large sums, you must know how to put that money to work for you. Investing in stocks naively or high-risk assets such as Bitcoin may leave you with less than you started.

Meet with a financial advisor, understand how to invest intelligently, and you'll be well on your way to visualizing success now.